This publication is offered for license under the Attribution Share-Alike license of Creative Commons, accessible at http://creativecommons.org/licenses/by-sa/4.0/legalcode and also described in summary form at http://creativecommons.org/licenses/by-sa/4.0/. By utilizing this Illustrated Scrum Guide, you acknowledge and agree that you have read and agree to be bound by the terms of the Attribution Share-Alike license of Creative Commons.

COPYRIGHT © 2020 ILKER DEMIREL

Visit our websites:
https://en.ilkerdemirel.com
https://www.leadershipmindset.de

Dear Reader,

I am happy that you like my work and hope you will have a great return on your investment.

If you are a big fan of illustrations while learning and teaching, you made an excellent choice. Congratulations!

You can use this Illustrated Scrum Guide to learn, teach and share your enthusiasm about agility and Scrum.

You have my permission to screenshot the pictures as they are and incorporate into your material. You can use it, even commercially, by just mentioning the reference as indicated in the licence agreement part.

As the Scrum is not prescriptive, the same is true also to this guide.
I trust on your mastery to build the right materials for yourself. As a Turkish saying indicates "Each hero has her way to eat yoghurt", you know the best way to use this material.
As a bonus, you are eligible to get a Scrum Training poster in high-resolution format (cf. last pages of this guide), which you can use in your online sessions, like in Miro.

Ilker Demirel, Dezember 2020, Berlin

Content

Manifesto*	46	Product backlog	74
Scrum values	47	Sprint backlog	76
Sprint	48	Increment	78
Sprint planning	50	Sprint goal	80
Sprint planning cont.	52	Definition of "done" (DoD)	82
Daily scrum	54	Five phases of a retrospective*	84
Sprint review	56	Impediment backlog*	86
Sprint retrospective	58	Planning poker*	88
Product backlog refinement	60	Product vision*	90
Scrum master	63	Release planning (Optional)*	92
Product owner	67	Release burndown*	94
Developers	70	Sprint burndown*	96
Scrum Team	72	User story*	98

PRINCIPLES BEHIND THE AGILE MANIFESTO

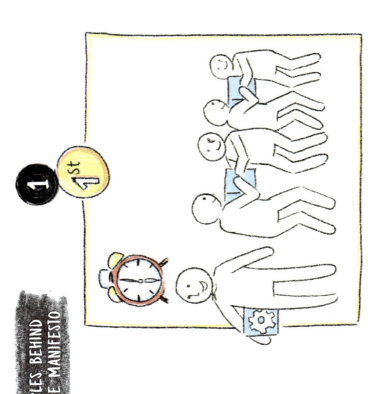

OUR HIGHEST PRIORITY IS TO SATISFY THE CUSTOMER THROUGH EARLY AND CONTINUOUS DELIVERY OF VALUABLE SOFTWARE.*

PRINCIPLES BEHIND THE AGILE MANIFESTO

2

WELCOME CHANGING REQUIREMENTS, EVEN LATE IN DEVELOPMENT.
AGILE PROCESSES HARNESS CHANGE FOR THE CUSTOMER'S COMPETITIVE ADVANTAGE.*

PRINCIPLES BEHIND THE AGILE MANIFESTO

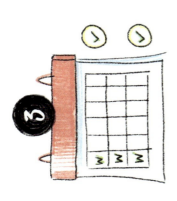

DELIVER WORKING SOFTWARE FREQUENTLY, FROM A COUPLE OF WEEKS TO A COUPLE OF MONTHS, WITH A PREFERENCE TO THE SHORTER TIMESCALE.*

PRINCIPLES BEHIND THE AGILE MANIFESTO

4

BUSINESS PEOPLE AND DEVELOPERS MUST WORK TOGETHER DAILY THROUGHOUT THE PROJECT.*

BUILD PROJECTS AROUND MOTIVATED INDIVIDUALS. GIVE THEM THE ENVIRONMENT AND SUPPORT THEY NEED, AND TRUST THEM TO GET THE JOB DONE.*

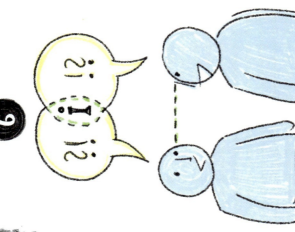

PRINCIPLES BEHIND THE AGILE MANIFESTO

THE MOST EFFICIENT AND EFFECTIVE METHOD OF CONVEYING INFORMATION TO AND WITHIN A DEVELOPMENT TEAM IS FACE-TO-FACE CONVERSATION.*

WORKING SOFTWARE IS THE PRIMARY MEASURE OF PROGRESS.*

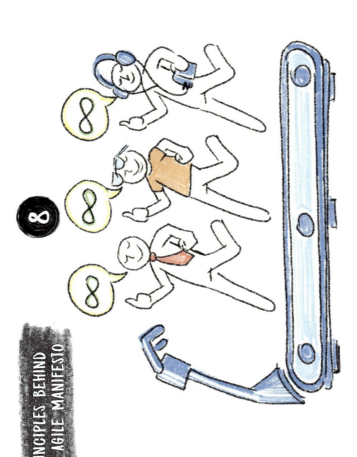

PRINCIPLES BEHIND THE AGILE MANIFESTO

AGILE PROCESSES PROMOTE SUSTAINABLE DEVELOPMENT. THE SPONSORS, DEVELOPERS, AND USERS SHOULD BE ABLE TO MAINTAIN A CONSTANT PACE INDEFINITELY.*

PRINCIPLES BEHIND THE AGILE MANIFESTO

CONTINUOUS ATTENTION TO TECHNICAL EXCELLENCE AND GOOD DESIGN ENHANCES AGILITY.*

PRINCIPLES BEHIND THE AGILE MANIFESTO

10

SIMPLICITY — THE ART OF MAXIMIZING THE AMOUNT OF WORK NOT DONE — IS ESSENTIAL.*

PRINCIPLES BEHIND THE AGILE MANIFESTO

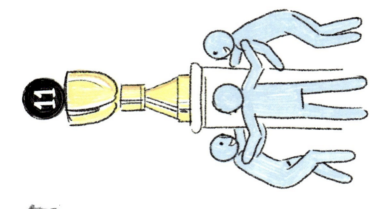

THE BEST ARCHITECTURES, REQUIREMENTS, AND DESIGNS EMERGE FROM SELF-ORGANIZING TEAMS.*

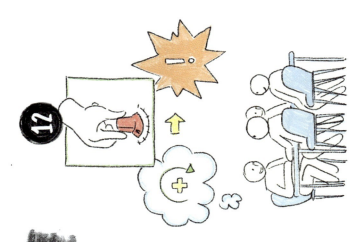

PRINCIPLES BEHIND THE AGILE MANIFESTO

AT REGULAR INTERVALS, THE TEAM REFLECTS ON HOW TO BECOME MORE EFFECTIVE, THEN TUNES AND ADJUSTS ITS BEHAVIOR ACCORDINGLY.*

- Inspect
- Adapt
- Transparency
- Scrum Framework is based on empirical process control

THREE PILLARS
OF EMPIRICAL PROCESS CONTROL AND SCRUM ARTIFACTS

PRODUCT GOAL — COMMITTED TO → PRODUCT BACKLOG

SPRINT GOAL — COMMITTED TO → SPRINT BACKLOG

DEFINITION OF DONE — COMMITTED TO → INCREMENT

SCRUM ARTIFACTS ARE TRANSPARENT, INSPECTED AND ADAPTED DURING THE **SPRINT**

SPRINT PLANING · DAILY SCRUM · SPRINT REVIEW · SPRINT RETROSPECTIVE

• continued

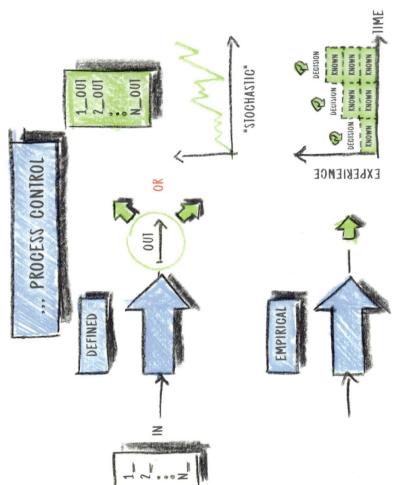

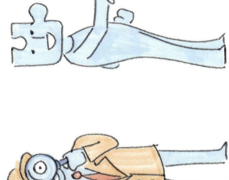
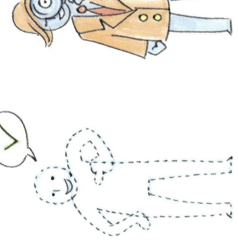

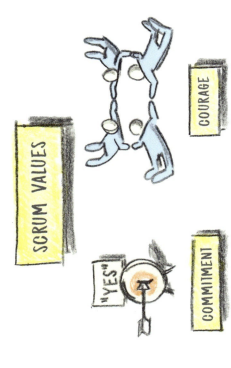

SCRUM FRAMEWORK

SPRINT GOAL

PRODUCT GOAL

SPRINT BACKLOG

SPRINT PLANNING

DAILY SCRUM

SPRINT

SPRINT RETROSPECTIVE

SPRINT REVIEW

INCREMENT

DEFINITION OF DONE

PRODUCT BACKLOG

DEVELOPERS (DEVS)
SCRUM MASTER (SM)
PRODUCT OWNER (PO)

ARTIFACTS
EVENTS

PRODUCT BACKLOG REFINEMENT (PBR)
UPDATE SPRINT BACKLOG
COMMITTED TO

ILKER D. DEMIREL

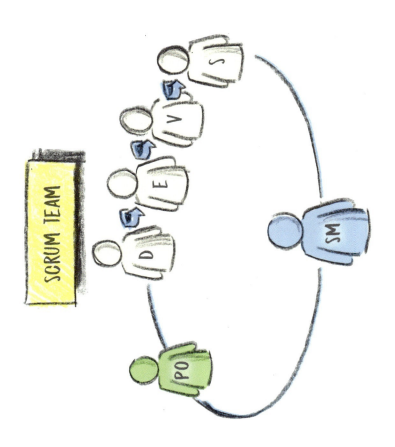

Credit to: Roman Pichler

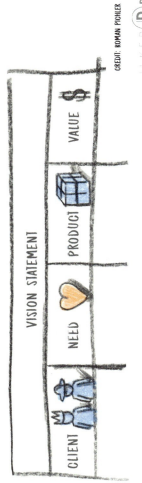

- Detail level vs. Priority
- Release Burndown*
- Sprint Burndown*
- Ownership
- **D**etailed appropriately, **E**stimated, **E**mergent and **P**rioritized **(DEEP)**

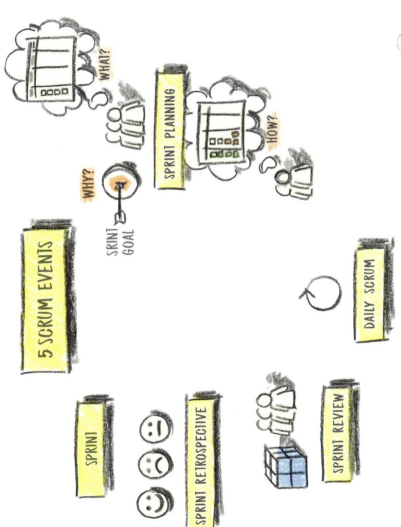

- Story template
- 3C
- INVEST

- Fibonacci
- Relative estimation

Credit to: Boris Gloger

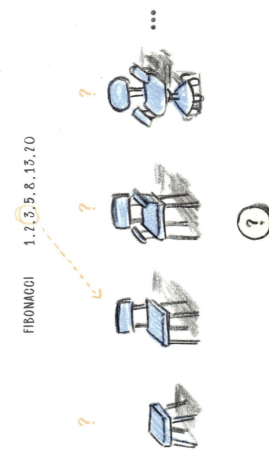

MANIFESTO *
FOR AGILE SOFTWARE DEVELOPMENT

We are uncovering better ways of developing software by doing it and helping others do it. Through this work we have come to value:

Individuals over interactions over processes and tools
Working software over comprehensive documentation
Customer collaboration over contract negotiation
Responding to change over following a plan

That is while there is value in the items on the right, we value the items on the left more.

http://agilemanifesto.org

SCRUM VALUES

Focus	Courage	Openness	Commitment	Respect
We focus on the work of the Sprint and the goals of the Scrum Team.	We have the courage to do the right thing and work on tough problems.	We all agree to be open about all the work and the challenges with performing the work.	We personally commit to achieving the goals of the Scrum Team.	We respect each other and we are capable, independent people.

SPRINT

Participants: Developers, Product Owner, Scrum Master
Focus: Achieve Sprint Goal and deliver Increment
Precondition: Product Backlog has been refined

- No requirement changes during Sprint that endanger Sprint Goal
- Quality goals remain constant.
- Sprint Planning executed and Daily Scrum meeting is held every day.
- Product Backlog Refinement is performed to prepare for next Sprint.
- Sprint Review meeting is held.
- Sprint Retrospective meeting is held after Sprint Review.

A ***Sprint*** is an iteration of work during which an Increment of product functionality is implemented, starting with Sprint Planning and ending with Sprint Retrospective. A Sprint immediately succeeds the preceding one. During a Sprint there are no changes allowed which would endanger the Sprint Goal.

Information on timing & scope ...

A Sprint is a fixed length of four weeks or less, preferably of the same length. This is the heartbeat of the Scrum.

Scope may be clarified and re-negotiated with the Product Owner as more is learned.

SPRINT PLANNING
"WHY IS THE SPRINT VALUABLE?"
"WHAT CAN BE DONE THIS SPRINT?"

Precondition: The input to this meeting is the refined Product Backlog, the latest product Increment, projected capacity of the Developers during the Sprint, and Definition of Done past performance of the Developers.

Participants: Scrum Team

- Acceptance criteria are clear for each Product Backlog item for this Sprint.
- Developers provide forecast which Product Backlog items will be delivered in this Sprint.
- Sprint Goal agreed, documented, and crafted by Scrum Team.

Sprint Planning is the first step of the sprint planning activity. The Product Owner presents the ordered Product Backlog items and the entire Scrum Team collaborates about understanding the work to be done in the Sprint. Afterwards the Developers forecast which items it can deliver in the next Sprint and the Scrum Team crafts a Sprint Goal. The following question is answered here: What can be delivered in the Increment resulting from the upcoming Sprint? Why is this Sprint valuable?

Information on timing ...

Sprint Planning is a timebox of altogether eight hours at maximum for a four-week Sprint. For shorter Sprints the event is usually shorter.

SPRINT PLANNING
"HOW WILL THE CHOSEN WORK BE DONE?"

Precondition: Forecast of Product Backlog and Sprint Goal

Participants: Developers, (optional Scrum Master, Product Owner)

- All Product Backlog items in Sprint decomposed into smaller tasks.
- Work planned for the first days of the Sprint by the Developers is decomposed by the end of this meeting, often to units of one day or less.

Sprint Planning cont. The Developers plan in detail which tasks are necessary to fulfill the Sprint Goal and deliver the forecasted Product Backlog items. The following question is answered here: How will the chosen work get done?

DAILY SCRUM

Participants: Developers, (If Scrum Master or Product Owner actively working in the Sprint Backlog, they participate as Developers)

Focus: Inspect progress toward the Sprint Goal, progress in achieving daily commitments, identify impediments

- Daily Scrum is every day: same place, same time, max. 15 min.
- All Developers members participate.
- Developers members are responsible for the event.

Considering it as a 15-minute event for the Developers to synchronize activities and create a plan for the next day. The Developers use the Daily Scrum to inspect progress toward the Sprint Goal and to inspect how progress is trending toward completing the work in the Sprint Backlog.

During the Sprint the Developers meet every day. In the **Daily Scrum** the Developers inspect the progress and ensure the communication flow within the Developers. The Daily Scrum is held at the same time and place each day to reduce complexity.

Information on timing ...

Daily Scrum is a short 15 minutes daily. It is held at the same time and place to reduce complexity.

Recommended techniques* ...

- Impediment Backlog
- Sprint Burndown

SPRINT REVIEW

Precondition: Increment is available

Participants: Product Owner, Developers, Stakeholder, Scrum Master, optional: anyone interested

- Demonstration of all done Product Backlog items "done" (no powerpoint*).
- Only items that meet the Definition of Done are demonstrated.
- Scrum Team and other stakeholders provide feedback on Increment.
- Scrum Team collects new ideas for Product Backlog items.

A ***Sprint Review*** is held to inspect the outcome of the Sprint and adapt the Product Backlog at the end of the Sprint, if needed. The Scrum Team demonstrates the Increment with focus on the Sprint Goal according to the Definition of "Done". The Scrum Team and stakeholders collaborate about what was noticeable in the current Sprint and what to do next.

Information on timing ...

Sprint Review is a timebox of up to four hours in case of a four-week Sprint. For Sprints of lesser duration, the event is usually shorter.

SPRINT RETROSPECTIVE

Participants: Scrum Master, Developers, Product Owner.

- Sprint Retrospective is planned and performed directly after Sprint Review!
- A few improvement suggestions are identified for implementation in the next Sprint.

The purpose of the Sprint Retrospective is to:

- Inspect how the last Sprint went with regards to people, relationships, process, tools, and Definition of Done.
- Identify and order the major items that went well and potential improvements; and,
- Create a plan for implementing improvements to the way the Scrum Team does its work. They may be added to the Sprint Backlog.

In next Sprint: Scrum Master assures that prioritized improvements will be implemented. The Scrum Team might also decide to run an experiment.

In ***Sprint Retrospective*** the Scrum Team revises their previous way of work in order to make it more efficient and effective in the future. The Scrum Master encourages the Scrum Team to search for best practices and to identify improvement measures which will be implemented in the next Sprint.

Information on timing ...

Sprint Retrospective is a timebox of up to three hours for a four-week Sprint.
For Sprints of lesser duration, the event is usually shorter.

Recommended techniques* ...

- Five Phases of a Retrospective

PRODUCT BACKLOG REFINEMENT

Participants: Product Owner, Scrum Master, Developers, optional: Stakeholders

- Product Backlog Refinement is performed during each Sprint! And it is an on-going activity.
- Product Backlog items are ordered (highest priority at the top*).
- After Product Backlog Refinement, ordered Product Backlog items are "ready" for Sprint Planning (at least: size, detailed, testable*).
  - Size: relative size/complexity of Product Backlog items estimated by Developers (e.g. story points*).
  - Detailed: Product Backlog items are small enough to do in one Sprint.
  - Testable*: acceptance criteria defined for Product Backlog item*.

Product Backlog Refinement is the act of adding detail, estimates, and order to items in the Product Backlog. This is an on-going process in which the Scrum Team collaborates on the Product Backlog and its details. Product Backlog items can be updated at any time. Product Backlog items that can be "Done" by the Developers within one Sprint are deemed "Ready" for selection in a Sprint Planning.

Information on timing ...

How and when Product Backlog Refinement is done is decided by the Scrum Team.

Recommended techniques* ...

- Product Vision
- Release Planning
- Release Burndown
- Planning Poker

SCRUM MASTER

- Is accountable for the Scrum Team's effectiveness.
- Coaching the Scrum Team members in self-management and cross-functionality.
- Participate as Developers in Daily Scrum while actively working on items in the Sprint Backlog.
- Helping the Scrum Team focus on creating high-value Increments that meet the Definition of Done.
- Causing the removal of impediments to the Scrum Team's progress.
- Ensuring that all Scrum events take place and are positive, productive, and kept within the timebox.
- Helping the Product Owner find techniques for effective Product Goal definition and Product Backlog management.
- Helping the Scrum Team understand the need for clear and concise Product Backlog items.
- Helping the Product Owner establish empirical product planning for a complex environment.
- Facilitating stakeholder collaboration as requested or needed.
- Leading, training, and coaching the organization in its Scrum adoption.

- Planning and advising Scrum implementations within the organization.
- Helping employees and stakeholders understand and enact an empirical approach for complex work.
- Removing barriers between stakeholders and Scrum Teams.

The **_Scrum Master_** is responsible for the Scrum Framework. This person ensures the Scrum process is understood and followed. The Scrum Master supports the Scrum Team and the organization to adopt and to use Scrum. He or she removes impediments of the Scrum Team so it can deliver the Increment. The Scrum Master facilitates the Scrum Team by coaching, teaching and supporting it to create high-value products.

PRODUCT OWNER

- Orders the work for a complex problem into a Product Backlog.
- Accountable for maximizing the value of the product resulting from the work of the Scrum Team.
- Developing and explicitly communicating the Product Goal.
- Creating and clearly communicating Product Backlog items.
- Accountable for effective Product Backlog management.
- Ordering Product Backlog items.
- Ensuring that the Product Backlog is transparent, visible and understood.
- May do the Product Backlog management work or may delegate the responsibility to others.
- Entire organization must respect their decisions.

- One person, not a committee.
- May represent the needs of many stakeholders in the Product Backlog.
- Has the authority to cancel the Sprint.
- Ensures that attendees of Sprint Planning are prepared to discuss the most important Product Backlog items and how they map to the Product Goal.
- Proposes during the Sprint Planning how the product could increase its value and utility in the current Sprint.
- Participates as Developers in Daily Scrum while actively working on items in the Sprint Backlog.

The **Product Owner** is responsible for the ROI of the product. This person provides, orders and manages the requirements in the Product Backlog. By making the Product Backlog visible to everyone, the Product Owner ensures the Developers works on the "right things" from a business perspective. He or she identifies what has been done and what has not been done in a Sprint. The Product Owner is a person, not a committee and is authorized to make definite decisions about the product, its features and the order of implementation.

DEVELOPERS

- Committed to creating any aspect of a usable Increment each Sprint.
- Accountable for creating a plan for the Sprint, the Sprint Backlog.
- Accountable for instilling quality by adhering to a Definition of Done.
- Accountable for adapting their plan each day toward the Sprint Goal.
- Accountable for holding each other accountable as professionals.
- Select items from the Product Backlog to include in the current Sprint.
- Plan the work necessary to create an Increment that meets the Definition of Done.
- Decomposing Product Backlog items into smaller work items of one day or less.
- Responsible for the sizing of the work.
- Committed to the Sprint Goal.

The **Developers** are responsible for delivering an Increment in each Sprint. The Developers as a whole must have the skills to deliver the Increment. It is responsible for all estimates and it forecasts the Product Backlog items it will deliver during a Sprint. The Developers decide on how to build an Increment. Furthermore, it maintains the Sprint Backlog and monitors the progress towards the Sprint Goal.

SCRUM TEAM

- Turns a selection of the work into an Increment of value during a Sprint.
- Inspect the results with stakeholders and adjust for the next Sprint.
- Is expected to adapt the moment it learns anything new through inspection.
- Commits to achieving its goals and to supporting each other.
- Is open about the work and the challenges together with its stakeholders.
- They respect each other to be capable, independent people, and are respected as such by the people with whom they work.
- Its members have the courage to do the right thing, to work on tough problems.
- Consists of one Scrum Master, one Product Owner, and Developers.
- Does not have sub-teams or hierarchies.
- They are cross-functional, meaning the members have all the skills necessary to create value each Sprint.

- They are also self-managing, meaning they internally decide who does what, when, and how.
- Is small enough to remain nimble and large enough to complete significant work within a Sprint, typically 10 or fewer people.
- Is responsible for all product-related activities from stakeholder collaboration, verification, maintenance, operation, experimentation, research and development, and anything else that might be required.
- Manage their own work.
- Is accountable for creating a valuable, useful Increment every Sprint.
- Collaboratively creates the Sprint Plan.
- May invite other people to attend Sprint Planning to provide advice.
- Collaborates to define a Sprint Goal.
- During the Sprint Review it presents the results of their work to key stakeholders and discusses the progress toward the Product Goal.
- Uses Product Backlog as the single source of work.
- Creates a Definition of Done appropriate for the product.

PRODUCT BACKLOG

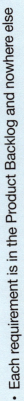

- Each requirement is in the Product Backlog and nowhere else
- Product Backlog is prioritized by Product Owner
- Top Product Backlog items are "ready" for Sprint Planning:
  - Refined and selected by Scrum Team
  - estimated by Developers
  - detailed enough to be implemented in one Sprint
  - formulated with acceptance criteria*
- Estimated Product Backlog is visible for Scrum Team
- The Product Backlog evolves as the product and the environment in which it will be used evolves.
- The Product Backlog lists all features, functions, requirements, enhancements, and fixes that constitute the changes to be made to the product in future releases. Product Backlog items have the attributes of a description, order, estimate, and value.

The **Product Backlog** is an ordered list of everything that might be needed for the product and is the single source of requirements for any changes to be made to the product. The Product Backlog is dynamic. Therefore it is constantly changed to identify the needs for the product to be adequate, competitive and useful. It is committed to Product Goal.

SPRINT BACKLOG

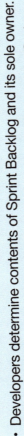

- Developers determine contents of Sprint Backlog and its sole owner.
- Sprint Backlog contains Product Backlog items selected for Sprint and the tasks needed to deliver.
- All work performed during a Sprint must be visible as a task on Sprint Backlog.
- Developers add, drop or detail tasks in Sprint Backlog as necessary.
- Developers add, drop or detail status of tasks in Sprint Backlog at least daily.
- Sprint Backlog is highly visible (e.g. on Scrum Board).
- Sprint Backlog emerges during the Sprint. This emergence occurs as the Developers work through the plan and learns more about the work needed to achieve the Sprint Goal.

The **Sprint Backlog** is the set of Product Backlog items selected for the Sprint including a plan for delivering the product Increment to achieve the Sprint Goal. The Sprint Backlog is a forecast done by the Developers on the functionality of the next Increment and the work needed to deliver functionality. It consists of Sprint Goal (why), Product Backlog Items selected for the Sprint (what), and plan to deliver the Increment (how). It is committed to Sprint Goal.

INCREMENT

- Delivered at end of Sprint.
- Complete slice of a final product.
- Potentially shippable (i.e. meets all requirements for delivery to an external stakeholder or customer).

The **Increment** is the sum of all Product Backlog items completed during the current Sprint and all previous ones. At the end of a Sprint the new Increment has to be in a usable condition and meet the Scrum Team's Definition of "Done". It is committed to Definition of Done.

SPRINT GOAL

- Sprint Goal is defined during Sprint Planning.
- Sprint Goal is visible in Sprint Backlog.
- Scrum Team maintains a focus on Sprint Goal during Sprint.

The **Sprint Goal** is an objective which will be met within the Sprint by implementing the forecasted Product Backlog items. It also provides guidance for the Scrum Team to focus on the expected results of the Sprint.

DEFINITION OF "DONE" (DOD)

- Definition of "Done" is visible and known to Scrum Team.
- DoD is generic and applies to all Product Backlog items in Sprint.
- DoD is agreed in Scrum Team.
- Specific Product Backlog items may have specific acceptance criteria*.
- Only items that meet DoD criteria are considered "Done".
- DoD guides the Developers in knowing how many Product Backlog items it can select during a Sprint Planning.
- If multiple Scrum Teams are working on one product release, then all Scrum Teams must mutually define a DoD.

The ***Definition of "Done"*** is a shared understanding of the Scrum Team on the meaning of work to be complete. It typically contains quality criteria, constraints, and overall non-functional requirements. As Scrum Teams mature, their Definition of "Done" is expected to expand encompassing more stringent criteria for higher quality. This ensures transparency.

FIVE PHASES OF A RETROSPECTIVE*

- Create an open atmosphere to be able to collect improvement suggestions.
- Collect information using appropriate techniques.
  - Starfish diagram (positive, negative experiences)
  - Timeline technique (what happened when)
- Perform analysis: "Why did things happen? What will we do differently?" (e.g. starfish diagram: do more, try, do less).
- Decide which improvement to implement in next Sprint.
- Document all results and close Retrospective.

The ***Five Phases of a Retrospective*** is a technique to facilitate a team to inspect its way of work and to identify actions to make it better. First, set the stage. Create an atmosphere where people feel comfortable discussing issues based on the understanding that everyone did the best job he or she could do, regardless of what went well and what did not. Second, gather data. This is often done by looking back and identifying what went well and what did not. Third, generate insights. In this phase, teams typically identify why things happened and what should be done more, less or given a try. Fourth, decide what to do. This includes deciding on specific, meaningful, agreed and realistic actions which will be done in the next Sprint. Fifth, close the retrospective. Decide how to document the results an plan for follow-up.

Credit to: Esther Derby and Diana Larsen.

IMPEDIMENT BACKLOG *

- Impediment Backlog is highly visible (e.g. on Scrum Board).
- Daily review of Impediment Backlog during Daily Scrum meeting.
- Scrum Master ensures resolution of impediments.

The *Impediment Backlog* is a technique for the Scrum Master to publicly collect all obstacles which impede the work. The Impediment Backlog is a list of impediments, tasks to resolve them and their current status.

PLANNING POKER *

FIBONACCI 1, 2, 3, 5, 8, 13, 20

- All estimation participants know "unit of measure": hours, days, story points, function points etc.
- In case of relative estimation: Every estimator knows reference item or story
- All participants estimate for themselves and turn their cards only after everyone has an estimate.
- If discussion leads to clarifications, definition of an item is updated accordingly
- Facilitator facilitates the process. For each item:
  - Step 1: Have story explained briefly + short round of clarifications
  - Step 2: Estimate for oneself
  - Step 3: Turn card and show
  - Step 4: Ask for the rationale from lowest and highest estimator
- Reiterate steps 2,3,4 until a consensus is reached.

Planning Poker is a consensus-based technique for estimating Product Backlog items or other things in Scrum. Usually, teams estimate the relative size of items. Planning Poker results in reliable and efficient estimations because the team gains a common understanding of the items. Planning Poker is a variation of the Wideband Delphi method.

PRODUCT VISION *

- Product Vision is documented and available to Scrum Team.
- Product Vision is short and precise.
- Everyone in the Scrum Team can state Product Vision.

A ***Product Vision*** is a technique to define the long-term goal of the project. It sets the overall direction and guides the Scrum Team. Everyone should be able to memorize the Product Vision; therefore it must be short and precise.

RELEASE PLANNING*
(OPTIONAL)

- Release Plan maintained by Product Owner.
- Release Plan updated during Product Backlog Refinement.
- Next release goal defined.
- Product Backlog items for next release are defined.
- Release Burndown updated.

Release Planning is a technique to order the realization of the product into releases and to forecast delivery dates. It establishes the goals of the release and the highest priority Product Backlog items describing the overall features and functionality which the release will contain.

A release is an increment that is transitioned into routine use by customers. Releases typically happen when one or more sprints resulted in the product having enough value to outweigh the cost to deploy it. The release plan establishes the goals of the release. The forecast is based on the team's velocity and estimations of the items in the release.

RELEASE BURNDOWN *

- Maintained by Product Owner.
- Updated during Product Backlog Refinement.
- Updated during the Sprint Review.

The **Release Burndown** is a technique to publicly display the progress of the current release. Typically a Release Burndown graph is used. The remaining work for a release is displayed on the vertical axis while the Sprints of a release are shown on the horizontal axis. Every Sprint the Product Owner updates the Release Burndown based on the velocity and the estimations of the team. Often the Release Burndown is used for the complete product showing the Burndown for all releases.

SPRINT BURNDOWN *

- Maintained by Developers.
- Updated daily at the end of Daily Scrum.

The Sprint Burndown is a technique to display the progress of the current Sprint publicly. Typically a Sprint Burndown graph is used. The remaining work in a Sprint is displayed on the vertical axis while the work days of a Sprint are shown on the horizontal axis. In the Daily Scrum the Developers update the Sprint and plots the remaining work of the day.

USER STORY *

```
AS A      <USER>
I WANT    <DESIRE>
SO THAT   <BENEFIT>
```

- User Story syntax:
  - As a ... [user] ...
  - I want ... [desire] ...
  - So that ... [benefit] ...
- Product Owner is responsible for writing user stories. PO may ask for support to write stories from the Developers.
- User stories are short and precise.

User stories are a technique to describe requirements from the perspective of a user utilizing everyday language. In Scrum User Stories can be used as Product Backlog items. The Product Owner writes them. A User Story captures what the user wants to achieve and why he or she wants it. User Stories follow this template: "As a USER I want GOAL/DESIRE so that BENEFIT." A User Story should be short and precise and fit on a small note card. User Stories provide a simple and easy way of handling customer requirements which can be product or service requirements. User Stories intend to capture the requirements quickly and to refine and break them down iteratively.

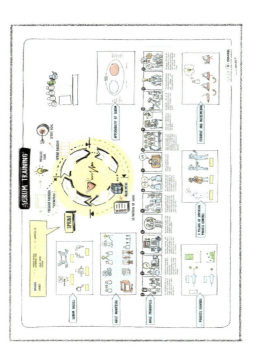

As an Illustrated Scrum Guide buyer, you are eligible to get a digital template to use in your Agile/ Scrum Training.
Please send an e-mail to ilker@ilkerdemirel.com with the Title "ILKERS_TEMPLATE_FOR_AGILE_SCRUM_TRAINING". You will receive a link to the template to download. You can use it in e.g. in Miro.

Ilker Demirel is Founder and CEO of ausculto GmbH and the first and only Certified Scrum Trainer (CST®) in the world delivering Certified ScrumMaster (CSM®) and Certified Product Owner (CSPO®) Training in English, German, and Turkish.

Ilker is helping organisations on having successful agile transformation, building high-performance teams, and effective agile leadership.

ausculto® GmbH
Ilker Demirel
Bergmannstr. 58
10961 Berlin

www.ilkerdemirel.com
ilker@ilkerdemirel.com

Geschäftsführer: Ilker Demirel
Registergericht: Amtsgericht Charlottenburg.
HRB 137107 B
Sitz der Gesellschaft: Berlin

© Ilker Demirel
Illustration: Miłosz Kasper Wachulski

ISBN 978-3-00-067818-9

This Illustrated Scrum Guide is based on the scrum guide November 2020 by Jeff Sutherland and Ken Schwaber
* not part of the official Scrum Guide; recommended technique and/or information; or taken from http://agilemanifesto.org

Printed in Poland
by Amazon Fulfillment
Poland Sp. z o.o., Wrocław